Winter 1981   Volume IV Number 4

Paperback Quarterly

"Journal of
Mass-Market Paperback History"

Contents

Paperback Quarterly Publications
Brownwood, Texas

Paperback Quarterly specializes in the history of mass market paperbacks. Its goal is to make the study of paperback history more comprehensive and reliable.

Paperback Quarterly features articles and notes dealing with every type (mystery, detective, science fiction, western, adventure, etc) and with every aspect of new, old and rare paperbacks.

Emphasis is place on the historical research of paperbacks, their authors, illustrators, publishers and distributors, but the editors also invite contributions of bibliographical interest. In short, the only criterion for the editors' consideration is that the subject matter pertain to paperbacks.

Paperback Quarterly pays 2¢ per word (200-2000 words) for articles and notes. Payment also includes two copies of the issue in which your article appears.

Paperback Quarterly is published in spring, summer, fall and winter of each year with a subscription rate of $10.00 per year or individual copies for $3.50 each. Institutional and library subscriptions are $12.00 per year. Overseas rate is $15.00. All back issues are out of print.

All correspondence, articles, notes, queries, ads and subscriptions should be sent to 1710 Vincent, Brownwood, Texas 76801. (915) 643-1182.

ad rate card on request.

Published and Edited by

Charlotte Laughlin   Billy C. Lee

Contributing Editors

Bill Crider   Michael S. Barson
William Lyles   Thomas L. Bonn
Piet Schreuders

Printer and Technical Advisor
Martin E. Gottschalk

Copy Editor
Judy Crider

Cover logo designed by Peter Manesis

Leon Shimkin — Paperback Pioneer
by Michael S. Barson

Leon Shimkin, one of the three men responsible for founding Pocket Books and officially beginning the paperback revolution, began his career in publishing almost as an accident. Looking for a summer job between semesters at NYU's School of Commerce in 1924, Shimkin applied to the firm of Boni & Liveright. In his interview with Arthur Pell, the firm's business manager, Shimkin explained that he could render any service that might be required of him--bookkeeping, stenography, collections, or even answering the switchboard. Impressed, Pell took the 17-year-old on at $25 a week. So well did Shimkin follow through on his pinch-hitting that Pell advised him of an opening at the new house of Simon & Schuster. Max Schuster's job offer forced Shimkin to finish his college education at night. So small an operation was Simon & Schuster in those days that Shimkin often had to deliver books on his way home from the office.

While it was Robert de Graff who originated the notion of a mass-produced line of paperbacks in the late '30s, Shimkin "midwifed" the idea, until, on June 19, 1939, the line made its official debut. But Pocket Books might never have become a reality had Shimkin not applied the technique of research and development to the project, coming up with the idea of test-marketing an edition of Pearl Buck's THE GOOD EARTH in August of 1938 in order to learn if the format of Pocket Books was appealing both to readers and book dealers. The answer was "yes" on both counts, and the results are familiar to anyone who has ventured into a bookstore or newsstand during the last forty-odd years.

Leon Shimkin went on to originate other profitable ideas for Simon & Schuster, including the legendary Little Golden Book line that

debuted in 1943. And it was Shimkin who
approached lecturer Dale Carnegie and, over his
protests, insisted on publishing what would
eventually become one of the best-selling self-
help books of all time, HOW TO WIN FRIENDS AND
INFLUENCE PEOPLE. Today the one-time president
of Simon & Schuster is semi-retired. But twice
a week he still shows up to make certain that
the Pocket Books empire--today the second-
largest in the country--is running smoothly.
Any midwife worth his salt would do as much to
look in on the welfare of his first-born child.

(Based in part on John Tebbel's 1966 SATUR-
DAY REVIEW article, "Leon Shimkin: The
Businessman As Publisher")

Interview with Leon Shimkin
Conducted by Michael S. Barson, December 1979

MB: Pearl Buck's THE GOOD EARTH was the book chosen as the vehicle for Pocket Books' 1938 experimental release. How was your campaign devised? What audience was exposed to this experiment, and how was it chosen?

LS: We issued THE GOOD EARTH by mail, asking people whether they liked the idea of a book of this size and look. And we got a very satisfactory answer. We got names by collecting lists of Book-of-the-Month Club members and people who regularly bought books from Brentano's and Scribner's. They responded with cards we had inserted. This encouraged us to embark on a program of ten more books, to be sold only in New York City, beginning in June, 1939.

MB: How were these editions promoted in New York? You had to make the public aware of Pocket Books' existence in some manner.

LS: We had a product that was readily visible at points-of-sale--namely, the newsstands. Once we found that our trial locations were doing good business, we printed more copies and approached more wholesalers. Finally we decided the simplest thing would be to take out a full-page ad in the New York TIMES announcing what we called "a revolution in book publishing." People all over the country started calling up morning, noon and night; they wanted to join the revolution! It took us a while to catch up with the demand we had created.

MB: Once you decided to gear up for production and distribution on a national scale, an

entirely new set of problems must have con-
fronted you, since you were marketing a
product that had not actually existed before.
How did you solve these problems?

LS: After New York we went from town to town
using mass distribution. Mass distribution
hadn't been used before for books, because
books were confined to bookstores, and there
were not many bookstores. We decided to use
the magazine wholesaler as the source of
distribution, figuring that where other
reading matter was bought, books would be
bought. And we were right. We used 750
wholesalers, which was enough for the time
being. However, the mass-distribution system we employed in 1939 and 1940 was very
small compared to today's system.

MB: Why didn't you try marketing Pocket Books in
bookstores? After all, they were books. Or
didn't the bookstores want to carry them?

LS: The reason we did not succeed in developing
Pocket Books' sales in bookstores is very
simple: the bookstores said, "Why spend the
time, energy and overhead trying to sell a
25¢ item, when we can sell a $5 or $10 item?
Include me out!" Of course, today that has
changed, since the price of paperbacks has
gone high enough to make carrying them worthwhile.

MB: Perhaps the bookstores also feared that a
paperback edition of a title would render
the hardcover version obsolete or unsaleable.

LS: It would seem that they should have resisted,
but actually we encountered no resistance.
The average bookseller was not concerned,
because to him it was a whole other business;

newspapers, magazines and paperbacks were
one thing, books were another.

But let me tell you a story. One of our
salesmen, Larry Hoyt, some ten years before
we began Pocket Books, asked if he could
conduct an experiment. He wanted to build
a lending library on the ground floor of
Filene's [department store] in Boston, on
the theory that, with the customers having
to walk through the whole store once to
borrow the book, and again to return it, the
store would gain a lot of traffic. This
experiment worked so well that, within ten
years, Larry had over a hundred department
stores all over the United States outfitted
with lending libraries. Then, in the tenth
year, he calls me up to tell me, "I want
to thank you for having helped me go into
business, Leon--and curse you for putting me
out of business! People would rather buy
your Pocket Books than rent mine!" I said,
"Take it easy... Let's put some Pocket Books
in some of your outlets and see how they do."
And this worked out very well.

Larry Hoyt, who's now retired, went on to
become the head of the Walden Books chain,
all of which have walls filled with paperbacks.

MB: It probably has an obvious explanation, but
I've always wondered why Pocket Books were
made in the size they were--a size which
most other paperback companies adhered to
well into the 1950's.

LS: We couldn't find a printer willing to print
our books at first; our way of binding would
have disrupted the operations of most
presses. But after some research we found

a plant in Clinton, Massachusetts called
the Colonial Press. They had an old press
which had a small cylinder. The limit of
this cylinder turned out to be the size
Pocket Books became. We matched that with
the "perfect binding" process, which had
been used for magazines, and ended up with
the product you know.

MB: The 25¢ price you began with--and adhered to
for almost fifteen years--also became the
accepted standard for the paperback houses
that followed Pocket Books. How did you
arrive at this cost, and how much did it
cost you to produce a Pocket Book in the
1940's?

LS: We arrived at the 25¢ price by allowing 5¢
to 8¢ to make the book; at that time paper
was very inexpensive. We also allowed 3¢
for the royalty and 5¢ for returns. There
was a certain amount allowed for advertising,
for promotion, and for overhead.

At first we had no problems at all; we made
a profit. And we wanted to sell to the
masses at the lowest possible price, rather
that the highest. Later on, some of our
competitors found it difficult to make it at
25¢ and had to raise the price to 35¢. We
refused to; we wanted to stay at 25¢. But
we found that the wholesaler preferred the
35¢ book and the 50¢ book, because they
could make extra money using the same amount
of stock and space. So we had to go along.

MB: Those must have been exciting times, estab-
lishing an entirely new format for books and
watching the public accept it with enthusiasm.

LS: I was so proud of our Pocket Books. Once, in

8

1939, I walked through Grand Central Station and saw my bright, new Pocket Books on display. I proudly said to the man, "Can I have a Pocket Book, please?" And he looked at me, puzzled, and said, "Around the corner; Ladies Handware." That was the beginning of Pocket Books.

Early Pocket Book Colophons

Ace Science Fiction Special Series
by Bill Crider

If you were going to start collecting science fiction books today and you wanted to begin
with paperbacks (but not new ones), where would
you begin? That's a tricky question. Almost
anything in the SF genre is collectible, it
seems, and finding good copies at reasonable
prices isn't easy. But one place to start
might be with the Ace Science Fiction Specials.
These books, published within the last 15
years, still turn up in used book stores at
half price. And in good condition. Besides,
if you like to read your collection, they pro-
vide some of the best entertainment anywhere.
And the covers, many of them by Leo and Diane
Dillon, are distinguised and distinctive.

One of my favorites in the series is Ron
Goulart's AFTER THINGS FELL APART, one of the
best combinations of science fiction and the
detective story that I've read. As usual with
Goulart's work, the whole thing is wild and
crazy; but, contrary to the title's implications,
it all holds together. In this book, Goulart's
unique combination of wit, satire, and story-
telling mesh perfectly, and the result is one
of the best things Goulart has done.

Of course, Goulart didn't win any of the
heavyweight awards for his book, but Ursula
LeGuin did the THE LEFT HAND OF DARKNESS,
copping both the Hugo and the Nebula. LeGuin
had been doing books for Ace for some time,
beginning with half of an Ace Double (G-574),
ROCANNON'S WORLD, but it was really THE LEFT
HAND OF DARKNESS that established her reputation
as one of the most interesting of contemporary
writers -- in any genre.

Another award winner was Alexei Panshin's
RITE OF PASSAGE (Nebula), Panshin's first novel

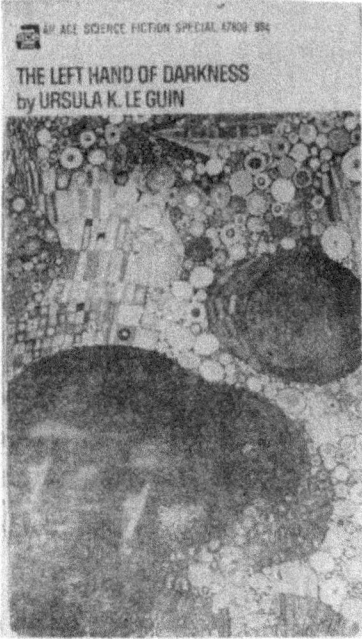

THE LEFT HAND OF DARKNESS
by URSULA K. LE GUIN

AN ACE SCIENCE FICTION SPECIAL

Leo & Diane Dillon

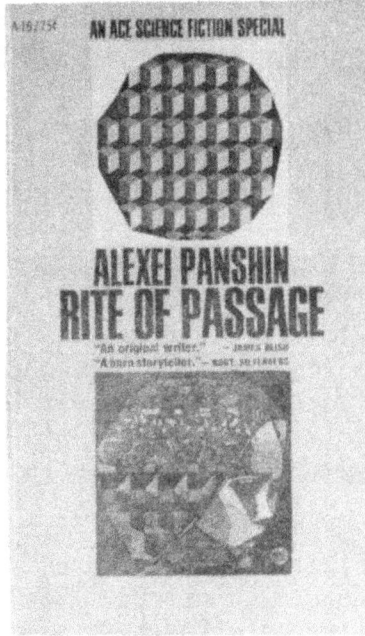

AN ACE SCIENCE FICTION SPECIAL

ALEXEI PANSHIN
RITE OF PASSAGE

Leo & Diane Dillon

AN ACE SCIENCE FICTION SPECIAL
THE TRAVELER IN BLACK
JOHN BRUNNER

Leo & Diane Dillon

FOURTH MANSIONS by R.A. LAFFERTY

AN ACE SCIENCE FICTION SPECIAL

Leo & Diane Dillon

Ace Science Fiction Specials

and (I think) his best. I haven't heard much from Panshin lately, which is a shame, because this book is truly deserving of its fame. Few male writers can tell a story from a woman's point of view as skillfully and well, and I hope for Panshin's comeback soon.

Wilson (Bob) Tucker's YEAR OF THE QUIET SUN also won an award, the Campbell Award (retrospectively). Besides being an excellent time-travel story, this is a "socially relevant" novel that actually works well as a novel. Tucker has done several memorable books, but this is one of his best.

Other books in the Ace SF Specials series are as good as those mentioned above. Keith Roberts's stately PAVANE is a reprint (all other books discussed are originals), but it is not to be missed. Set in an England of an alternate Earth (the Spanish Armada is victorious on this Earth), PAVANE is literature of a high order, a fine and absolutely convincing work of the imagination.

Also worth consideration is John Brunner's THE JAGGED ORBIT. Not as well known as Brunner's STAND ON ZANZIBAR, the book is nearly as successful, though it lacks the other's John Dos Passos style. One thing it does have, however, and this is fair warning, is outrageous puns for any number of its chapter titles. The book is absolutely serious, but funny at the same time. Another Brunner title in the series is THE TRAVELER IN BLACK, which you might call Sword & Sorcery, and you might not. I've never read anything quite like it by Brunner or anyone else; it's the kind of science fantasy that isn't easy to find.

And speaking of the kind of science fiction that isn't easy to find, there are two books by R. A. Lafferty in the series: PAST MASTER and FOURTH MANSIONS. Lafferty's work is of course unique and indescribeable, and I won't even try.

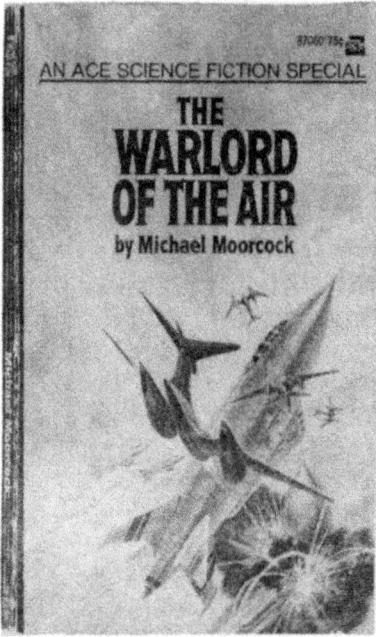

AN ACE SCIENCE FICTION SPECIAL

THE WARLORD OF THE AIR

by Michael Moorcock

Davis Meltzer

AN ACE SCIENCE FICTION SPECIAL

THE PRESERVING MACHINE
by PHILIP K. DICK

Leo & Diane Dillon

AN ACE SCIENCE FICTION SPECIAL

THE ISLAND UNDER THE EARTH
by AVRAM DAVIDSON

Leo & Diane Dillon

AN ACE SCIENCE FICTION SPECIAL

MECHASM by JOHN T. SLADEK

Leo & Diane Dillon

Ace Science Fiction Specials

But if you haven't read these books, you've missed some of the most unusual writing in the SF field. And probably some of the best.

You also shouldn't miss Michael Moorcock's THE BLACK CORRIDOR, the kind of science fiction that Moorecock apparently wanted to write when his Sword & Sorcery was so popular that no one wanted to buy anything else from him. And Moorcock's THE WARLORD OF THE AIR (incidentally the last book in the original series) will remain famous as the alternate earth novel (in this one, the Russian Revolution failed) in which Mick Jagger has a walk-on. As a London policeman.

Other books in the series? They're all worthwhile. Philip K. Dick's short story collection, THE PRESERVING MACHINE. Joanna Russ' PICNIC ON PARADISE. Avram Davidson's THE ISLAND UNDER THE EARTH. Roger Zelazny's ISLE OF THE DEAD. This series was edited by Donald Wollheim and Terry Carr and ended when they left Ace Books, despite a later attempt to revive it; it remains one of the more dis-tinguished series efforts in science fiction publishing history. Get it while you can.

The Destroyer Series
by Will Murray

In June 1971, Pinnacle Books, flushed with success over Don Pendleton's Executioner series, published a book called CREATED, THE DESTROYER by Richard Sapier and Warren Murphy. It was the first book in a new series inspired by the new action-adventure trend--even though the novel had been written in 1963!

The Destroyer story began when Sapir and Murphy, two New Jersey reporters, decided to write a novel, inspired by the James Bond craze sweeping America at that time. They wrote CREATED, THE DESTROYER in an attic, writing and rewriting one another's alternate chapters. By their own admission, they didn't know what they were doing, and so the novel went the rounds of agents and editors unsuccessfully. No one was buying series novels, they were told. In fact, there weren't any series novels being done-- which was partially true. They only sold the manuscript because Richard Sapir's father, a dentist, happened to mention the novel to one of his patients, a Pinnacle secretary, who brought it to the attention of the series-hungry new publisher.

CREATED, THE DESTROYER is the deadpan story of Remo Williams, Newark cop who is framed for a murder by America's supersecret law-enforcement agency, CURE, supposedly executed, but really recruited to be CURE's enforcement arm -- an assassin empowered to act outside the law in order to preserve it. His eighty year old trainer, Chiun, is a Korean karate master, who gives Remo the abilities to carry out CURE's orders. This was nothing new in popular fiction, especially by the time it was published.

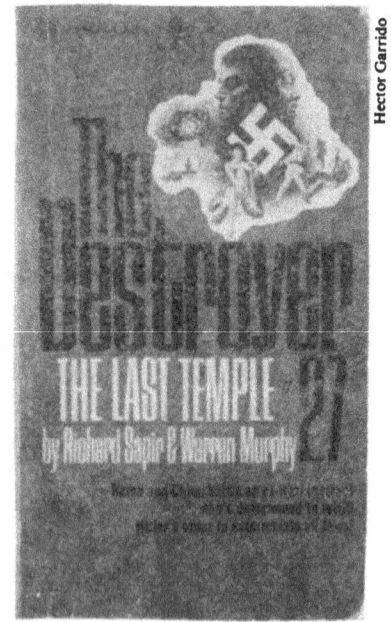

Hector Garrido

The Destroyer Series

When Sapir and Murphy received their contract for a sequel, DEATH CHECK, they decided
to update the character, turn him into a super-
man of sorts and write Chiun into the background. DEATH CHECK, like CREATED, THE DESTROY-
ER, are, in the writers' own opinions, false
starts.

DEATH CHECK was published as #2 in the
Destroyer series, which came as a shock to its
authors; the Destroyer name was part of the
first title, a quote from the Bagavad Gita, and
not meant to be the character's name. Worse,
their editors wanted them to write the series
in emulation of the Executioner, with blood and
bodies galore. They balked, got drunk and
planned the third book, CHINESE PUZZLE. With
this book, the series really begins.

With CHINESE PUZZLE, Chiun re-enters the
series as a humorous, kvetching father-figure
for Remo. Remo's abilities are broadened; and,
taking advantage of the situation, the authors
hint that he may be the reincarnation of the
Hindu god, Shiva the destroyer. In this novel,
Sinanju is also introduced. It is the North
Korean village from where Chiun hails, but it is
also the home of a house of legendary assassins
who have hired themselves out since before the
Pharaohs. Chiun is the latest of the Masters
of Sinanju--never mind that he talks and acts
like a Jewish mama. In succeeding novels, the
history of Sinanju--which is also the source of
all forms of martial arts--is explored and refined.

Pinnacle's reaction to the humor and mythology was a stern order to Sapir and Murphy to
cut out the mythology and humor. They refused
and plowed ahead, expanding their horizons by
introducing political humor into the series.

With the fourth book, Sapir and Murphy
evolved what was to be their unique approach to
collaborating. Up until then, Sapir outlined

the novels and did most of the preliminary writing and Murphy polished and revised. In the middle of MAFIA FIX, Sapir decided he had writ-ten enough and turned the novel and outline over to Murphy, who completed it and did the final draft. From then on, that was the rule: Sapir did the first 95 pages and a brief out-line; Murphy did the finish and the final draft. Surprisingly, this approach worked beautifully.

The fifth book, DR. QUAKE, was nearly a catastrophe, however. Sapir outlined a death scene in which Chiun sacrifices his life for his adopted pupil, Remo, who becomes the new Master of Sinanju. Murphy balked at this and convinced Sapir that this would be a great mis-take. Sapir relented, which was fortunate for the series, as Chiun grew to be the brain of the team.

After DR. QUAKE, a temporary rift developed between Sapir and Murphy, which resulted in their writing the next two books solo. Although they carry double bylines, UNION BUST is by Richard Sapir and SUMMIT CHASE is Warren Murphy's. A comparison of the brooding Sapir novel and the comical Murphy novel show their comparative strengths and weaknesses. Richard Sapir's forte is plot and characterization, while Murphy excels at action and a broad humor he says was inspried by the Doc Savage novels he read as a child. Of the two, SUMMIT CHASE is closer to a typical Destroyer novel; but UNION BUST introduces Nuich, Chiun's evil first pupil and the first recurring villain in the series; it also has one of the great bits in the series in which Remo eats a fast-food hamburger and nearly dies because his training has so purified his system that he can no longer eat junk foods!

The ninth book, MURDER'S SHIELD, suffers from the fact that, although it was a collabor-ation, the two writers were not speaking to one another. Sapir wrote the first half, but no

18

outline, and Murphy's finish does not show much
enthusiasm. But with TERROR SQUAD, the series
is back to normal. And Nuich is back, too. He
returned again in OIL SLICK and finally in
ASSASSINS PLAY-OFF, in which Remo and Chiun
visit the village of Sinanju to fight Nuich to
the death. ASSASSINS PLAY-OFF is probably the
peak of the series to date, in terms of sheer
writing and plot.

A second recurring villain, an android
named Mr. Gordons (after the scotch) showed up
in FUNNY MONEY and returned in BRAIN DRAIN.
Whereas Nuich was a serious foe, Gordons was
played for laughs, albeit he was equally deadly.
When initial mail response seemed to indicate
readers didn't like Gordons, he was dropped
from the series; but subsequent letters have
demanded his return, and a third match with the
android is planned for book #48.

Despite Pinnacle's initial objections to
the satirical and mythological aspects of the
series, The Destroyer flourished--in fact,
these elements are precisely what set it above
all other series.

After an initial spurt, the authors settled
down to writing four books per year. Pinnacle,
however, wanted six per year. Richard Sapir
was more interested in doing books on his own,
so Warren Murphy hired a young writer named
Richard S. Meyers to collaborate on alternative
novels in 1976. Working from Murphy's outlines,
Meyers wrote SWEET DREAMS (#25), THE LAST
TEMPLE (#27) and THE FINAL DEATH (#29). Although the resulting novels were good (Murphy
himself did the final drafts), Murphy found the
pace more than he cared for, and the series went
back to four books a year.

By this time, the satirical bent of the
series was strong and beginning to attract
readers outside of the action-adventure genre,
as well as winning over those who didn't like

the first two books in the series. Among the headline items raked over the coals by Sapir and Murphy were the Indian Movement (LAST WAR DANCE), gurus (HOLY TERROR) and race relations (MUGGER BLOOD). Public figures from Father Berrigan to Idi Amin were lampooned, as was one of The Destroyer's original inspirations--James Bond--in SUMMIT CHASE.

Specific types of Destroyer novels also emerged. Although most stories involved CURE missions, the rich Background Sapir and Murphy were evolving became the springboards for plots. Some revolved around the threatened exposure of CURE (KILL OR CURE and JUDGMENT DAY) or age-old menaces from Sinanju's past (THE FINAL DEATH and POWER PLAY). A surprising number of the novels are either science fiction or fantasy. Among the best of these are KILLER CHROMOSOMES and FIRING LINE.

Throughout the long run of the series, the writers kept busy with separate projects. Warren Murphy wrote the five book Razoni and Jackson series, about a pair of New Jersey cops, for Pinnacle in 1973. His locked room mystery, LEORNADO'S LAW, was published by Carlyle in 1978; and he did the screenplay to THE EIGER SANCTION. Richard Sapir wrote BRESSIO, a Mafia novel, for Random House in 1975; his 1978 mainstream science fiction novel, THE FAR ARENA, was very successful.

Sapir's success and his felling that he was growing stale on The Destroyer caused him to leave the series as co-author in 1978--but not before he created a new recurring character. In VOODOO DIE, ex-CIA agent Ruby Jackson Gonzales, was introduced. Ruby is a black woman inspired by Chrissie Negargel, Warren Murphy's policewoman girlfriend. Sapir invented the character, but it was Murphy who decided to make her a semi-regular. In the next novel, CHAINED REACTION, she joins CURE. Her appear-

The Destroyer Series

ances to date include LAST CALL, BOTTOM LINE, BAY CITY BLAST and FIRING LINE. In the latter book, she leaves the series as a regular. Reader reaction felt she was in the way of Remo and Chiun's father-son relationship. She may return in future books.

CHAINED REACTION was the last Sapir and Murphy collaboration to date, although the by-line was not changed until BAY CITY BLAST. This was done at Richard Sapir's suggestion, so that the novels would be put in the "M" sections of bookstores. It was an economic move, and even the backlist novels are being reissued under Warren Murphy's name only. Sapir, however, remained involved in the series. His plot ideas, research, even scenes and chapters have made their way into subsequent novels. For example, he wrote an introduction, signed by Chiun, for POWER PLAY. A similar Chiun intro-duction, warning the reader not to read CREATED, THE DESTROYER, was added to the 1976 reissue of that book. (It also featured an afterward by Richard Meyers, who went on to write other books on his own, including CRY OF THE BEAST, a novel featuring the Incredible Hulk; the DOOMSTAR books for Carlyle; and alternate books in the Ninja Master and Dirty Harry series.) Pinnacle wouldn't let Sapir and Murphy revise CREATED, THE DESTROYER--thus Chiun's introduction. The reissue is worth buying for the introduction alone.

Warren Murphy wrote the next five Destroyer novels alone. The quality did not drop. POWER PLAY was a satire on HUSTLER publisher Larry Flynt. MISSING LINK poked fun at Billy Carter and the Libyans--a novel that was actually written before that story broke in the papers, and one of the most interesting examples of popular fiction anticipating reality in recent times. One of Murphy's best Destroyers was his satire on Pinnacle's Executioner, Butcher, and Death Merchant. Samuel Gregory (a named cobbled

from two Don Pendleton psuedonyms) is the
villain of BAY CITY BLAST, (a deliberate
Executioner-style title) and he is assisted by
The Exterminator, The Baker and The Lizzard.
This is a savage send-up of the whole action-
adventure genre.

After about a year of solo novels, Murphy
began to feel the need for a new collaborator
and tried several. Both DANGEROUS GAMES and
MIDNIGHT MAN were written by Robert Randisi
from Murphy's outlines. Murphy, as always, did
the final drafts. Both novels had the misfor-
tune to run afoul of current events--DANGEROUS
GAMES took place at the Moscow Olympics where
the American boycott hadn't been heard of, and
MIDNIGHT MAN concerned Remo's attempts to pro-
tect the late Shah of Iran from assassination.
Robert Randisi has written under his own name
and contributes to the Nick Carter series.

One novel, TIMBER LINE, was the work of
William "Ted" Joy, who may be writing some of
the Executioner spin-off books for Harlequin.

The most recent, and promising, new writer
to undertake the series is a young woman named
Molly Cochran, who has written the tenth anni-
versary Destroyer, BALANCE OF POWER, from a
private detective novel called "Black Barney"
which Sapir and Murphy wrote and never sold in
the mid-sixties. Thus, this novel will appropriately have bits of Sapir, Murphy and Cochran.

Molly Cochran has already written three
Destroyers, and she is likely to remain with
the series for the near future. But the best
news of all may be this: Richard Sapir and
Warren Murphy have signed a new contract that
will take them up to book #68 (This was after
they turned down an incredible twenty-year
contract that would have committed them to four
Destroyers a year until the year 2000!) and
they have decided to collaborate on one Destroyer a year, just as they used to write--except

23

that these novels will be special. Not only
will they feature the old byline, but they will
be significantly longer, with even more attention paid to the characters who have made The
Destroyer a paperback phenomenon. On top of
that, Pinnacle will be issuing a trade paperback on the series, to be called THE ASSASSIN'S
HANDBOOK, which will feature articles, inter-
views, legends and other material on the
series, as well as a new Destroyer novelette by
Sapir and Murphy.

The Destroyer Index

1.	CREATED, THE DESTROYER	6/71	a*
2.	DEATH CHECK	1/72	a
3.	CHINESE PUZZLE	3/72	a
4.	MAFIA FIX	5/72	a
5.	DR. QUAKE	9/72	a
6.	DEATH THERAPY	10/72	a
7.	UNION BUST	1/73	b
8.	SUMMIT CHASE	2/73	c
9.	MURDER'S SHIELD	4/73	a
10.	TERROR SQUAD	6/73	a
11.	KILL OR CURE	8/73	a
12.	SLAVE SAFARI	9/73	a
13.	ACID ROCK	12/73	a
14.	JUDGMENT DAY	2/74	a
15.	MURDER WARD	4/74	a
16.	OIL SLICK	8/74	a
17.	LAST WAR DANCE	10/74	a
18.	FUNNY MONEY	2/75	a
19.	HOLY TERROR	6/75	a
20.	ASSASSINS PLAY-OFF	9/75	a
21.	DEADLY SEEDS	11/75	a
22.	BRAIN DRAIN	1/76	a
23.	CHILD'S PLAY	4/76	a
24.	KING'S CURSE	7/76	a
25.	SWEET DREAMS	10/76	d
26.	IN ENEMY HANDS	1/77	a

27.	THE LAST TEMPLE	3/77	d
28.	SHIP OF DEATH	5/77	a
29.	THE FINAL DEATH	7/77	d
30.	MUGGER BLOOD	9/77	a
31.	THE HEAD MEN	11/77	a
32.	KILLER CHROMOMSOMES	3/78	a
33.	VOODOO DIE	6/78	a
34.	CHAINED REACTION	9/78	a
35.	LAST CALL	12/78	c
36.	POWER PLAY	3/79	c
37.	BOTTOM LINE	7/79	c
38.	BAY CITY BLAST	10/79	c
39.	MISSING LINK	2/80	c
40.	DANGEROUS GAMES	5/80	e
41.	FIRING LINE	8/80	c
42.	TIMBER LINE	11/80	f
43.	MIDNIGHT MAN	2/81	e
44.	BALANCE OF POWER	5/81	g
45.	SPOILS OF WAR	8/81	g
46.	NEXT OF KIN	11/81	g
47.	DYING SPACE	2/82	g
48.	PROFIT MOTIVE	5/82	a
49.	SKIN DEEP	8/82	g

*Authors:
  a. Richard Sapir and Warren Murphy
  b. Richard Sapir
  c. Warren Murphy
  d. Richard S. Meyers and Warren Murphy
  e. Robert Randisi and Warren Murphy
  f. William "Ted" Joy and Warren Murphy
  g. Molly Cochran and Warren Murphy

Skeleton Covers

by Bill Crider

The hand of the Lord was upon me, and He brought me out by the Spirit of the Lord and set me down in the middle of the valley; and it was full of bones. --Ezekiel 37:1

At the 1981 Bouchercon in Milwaukee, just before Art Scott's remarkable slide show of paperback cover art, Bob Napier asked the members of the panel then in session if they were aware that some collectors specialized in certain motifs. He insisted that he even knew of someone who was collecting covers featuring dogs with money in their mouths. I found that a little hard to believe, but I started thinking. Obviously, beautifully fleshed female bodies were the number one paperback cover motif (see "Paperback Bodies," PQ, Winter 1979). But what was number two? It occured to me that number two was probably the exact opposite of number one, that of bodies with no flesh on them at all -- skeletons, of course.

Skeletons have been a favorite of paperback artists from almost the beginnings to the present. The 1943 Avon edition of Raymond Chandler's THE BIG SLEEP is probably the best-known early example, but Dell Books featured plenty of skeletons in the 1940s on such books as MURDER AND THE MARRIED VIRGIN (128), DEATH AND THE DOLL'S HOUSE (122), HOLIDAY HOMICIDE (22), THE MIRABILIS DIAMOND (303), THE LAST EXPRESS (95), FIRE WILL FREEZE (157), PICK YOUR VICTIM (307), MADE UP TO KILL (106), THE CROOKING FINGER (104), THE SMELL OF MONEY (219), THE CHARRED WITNESS (240), and MIDSUMMER NIGHTMARE (150). Actually a cursory examination of these books reveals that skeletons in their entirety are not pictured on any of them. What is generally shown is a skull or a pair of skeletal hands. Sometimes, the hands are gloved, as on PICK YOUR VICTIM, which also has a skull in the background. Sometimes,

Skeleton Covers

Bob Stanley

Phil Marini

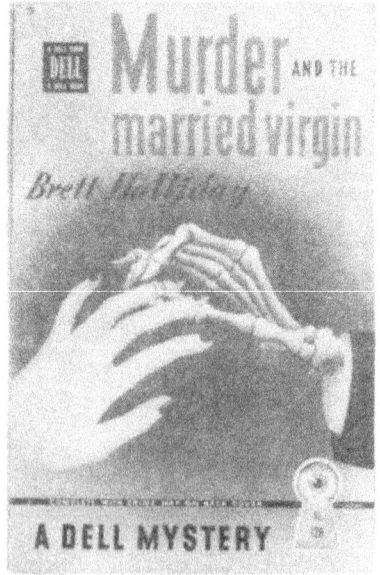

Skeleton Covers

28

the skull is adorned with hair as on THE BIG
SLEEP. Often the apparent skeleton is caped,
as on PICK YOUR VICTIM, FIRE WILL FREEZE, and
MIDSUMMER NIGHTMARE.

A nice variation on the cape and gloves
appears on the digest-sized edition (Complete
Novel Selections #6) of Lawrence Lariar's DEATH
IS THE HOST. On this vivid cover, a skeleton
in a white tie and tails (not to mention white
gloves) presides over a deadly dinner party.
Perhaps the other guests failed to dress
properly.

Other fine skeleton hands from the 1940s
can be found on such books as Popular Library
#31, MURDER BY THE CLOCK. Incidentally, the
author of this book is Rufus King, who wrote
HOLIDAY HOMICIDE. The top-hatted skull on the
latter cover looks as if it would be right at
home with the jolly host provided by the artist
for Lariar's book mentioned above, and that very
host might be the one whose now ungloved hands
are playing the piano for the well-dressed
dancers on Bart House #9, THE WALTZ OF DEATH.
The hand holding the dripping arrow on the
cover of THE JUDAS WINDOW (Pocket Books #231)
is probably no relation at all.

More complete skeletons, the ones who have
it all together, decorate the covers of books
like Bantam #51, DEATH IN THE BLACKOUT, in which
the bony fellow decides to lower his shade (no
pun intended). Dell 481, THE SKELETON IN THE
CLOCK, provides a cover with a quite literal
vision of the title incorporated into it. And
Dell 621, LAMENT FOR THE BRIDE, certainly gives
the bride on its cover something to think about;
she'd probably rather have her mother-in-law
along.

Skeletal hands made their way into the
1950s by playing a rock beat on the conga drums
of BEAT NOT THE BONES (Avon T-376). The woman
on the cover obviously doesn't appreciate the

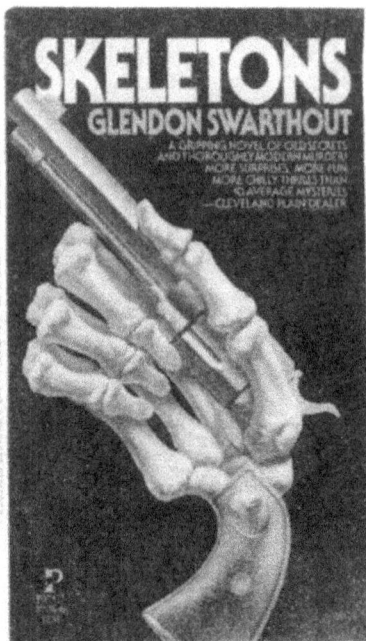

Skeleton Covers

Skeleton Cover featuring a die cut overlay

rhythm, or maybe she can see more than the
hands. Anyway, the hands aren't beating anyone's bones as the title might imply; they're
beating those drums.

All the books mentioned so far have been
mysteries, and skeletons prove to be very
popular on mystery covers even now. The great
skeleton hand gun (no pun intended) on the cover
of Glendon Swarthout's aptly titled SKELETONS
(Pocket Books, 1981) is one of the best covers
of its kind. Avon Books seems intent on pro-
moting the generally very funny (but only in
a genteel sort of way) mysteries of Charlotte
MacLeod with a series of skeleton covers for
her books about Professor Peter Shandy and
those involving Sarah Kelling. A prime example
is the cover of the first Shandy book (Avon,
1979), with its bizzare Santa and four of his
tiny reindeer. The very best recent example,
however, has to be the double cover for Judi
Miller's SAVE THE LAST DANCE FOR ME (Pocket
Books, 1981). The front cover shows a curtain
being parted by a bony hand and gives a glimpse
of a girl's face. The inside cover reveals the
girl, dressed in a tutu and held in the gruesome
grasp of Mr. Bones himself.

Another genre that would seem a likely
prospect for skeleton covers is that of horror
fiction. Oddly enough, there are not that many
examples to be found. THE HAUNTED DANCERS
(Paperback Library, 1967) does offer a ghastly
embrace between a living woman and a bony guy
in a shabby cape, and Robert Bloch's TALES IN
A JUGULAR VEIN (Pyramid, 1965) depicts what
apprears to be a robot skull (or a skull-like
robot) with a friend of Edgar Poe's perched
atop it. A more contemporary example is on the
cover of Fred Saberhagen's fourth novel in his
"new Dracula" series, THORN (which Saberhagen
says he originally titled A MATTER OF TASTE;
publishers don't like puns).

BEAT NOT THE BONES

"BEST MYSTERY OF THE YEAR" AWARD
Mystery Writers of America

Charlotte Jay
Complete and unabridged

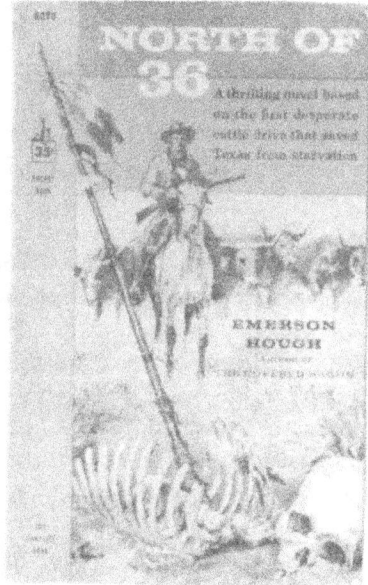

NORTH OF 36

A thrilling novel based on the last desperate cattle drive that saved Texas from starvation

EMERSON HOUGH

A HIGHLY ORIGINAL NOVEL OF HOW THE WEST WON

MONTANA GOTHIC

BY DIRCK VAN SICKLE

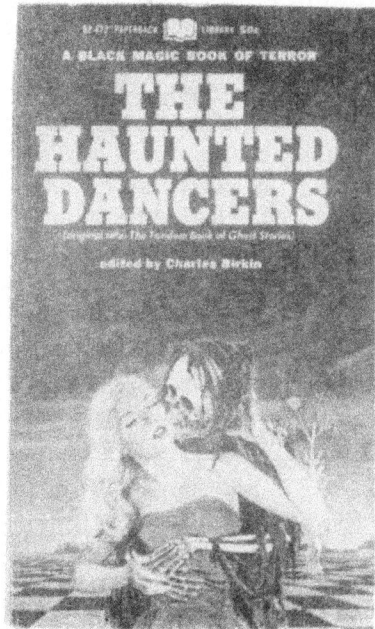

A BLACK MAGIC BOOK OF TERROR

THE HAUNTED DANCERS

edited by Charles Birkin

Victor Kalin

Skeleton Covers

Skeleton parts are sometimes found on science fiction books, too, but rarely in prominent positions. An exception is A PLAGUE OF DEMONS (Paperback Library, 1971) by Keith Laumer, which seems to be about "Giant robots with human brains...." They may be related to the cover model for Bloch's book for all I know. Michael Moorcock's Elric faces a sort of skeletal monster in the heroic fantasy world portrayed on THE BANE OF THE BLACK SWORD (DAW, 1977); it's interesting that Moorcock's THE JEWEL IN THE SKULL has no skull at all on either the cover of the Lancer edition (1967) or the DAW edition (1977). Two artists missed their big chance. THE EARLY DEL REY (Ballantine, 1976) makes up for this lack, though, by giving us two skulls to flank the sinister clown's face framed by the old portable typewriter, and THE BEST OF PLANET STORIES #1 (Ballantine, 1975) has a couple of skeletons in the background that would make Ray Harryhausen feel proud.

Skeletons are even more difficult to find in the field of Westerns. Cow bones might be lying around some poisoned water hole, but to find the real thing you have to look long and hard. Pocket Books 6070, NORTH OF 36 by Emerson Hough, is the best single example, with its graphic warning to settlers of what might wait for them in Indian country.

In mainstream fiction, there just aren't any skeletons, or if there are maybe someone will point them out to me later. There is, however, the unclassifiable MONTANY GOTHIC (Avon, 1980), by Dirck Van Sickle. We can only speculate that the author's wonderfully appropriate name led the artist to his inspiration, resulting in a far-from-urban cowboy with the best set of teeth around.

If I missed the favorite skeleton in your closet, let me know. Maybe I can do this again sometime.

34

Elements of Success
by Thomas L. Bonn

The 1940s and 1950s were littered with the
remains and remainders of mass market publishers,
many of them offshoots of magazine and magazine
distributing companies that did not make it
through the wars of competition. Among them
were Lion, Graphic, Bart, Anson Bond, Hillman,
Handi, Black Knight and, appropriately enough,
Bleak House. A brief examination of each of
the four basic elements for success in mass
market publishing is essential to the under-
standing of the industry's history. This essay
will outline each one and, for three of them,
describe present day publisher practice.

Distribution

Distribution is named most frequently as
the element that most accounts for the industry's
success. The goal of distribution is to reach,
first and foremost, the 150,000 plus retail
accounts--newstands, variety stores, convenience
stores, supermarkets and drugstores--that sell
paperback books in the United States and Canada.
These accounts are primarily serviced by independent wholesale distributors (IDs). Often
locally owned, these businesses usually have
exclusive distribution rights within a terri-
tory to retail stores (with the exception of
bookstores and some chain stores) for out-of-
town newspapers, mass circulation magazines,
tabloids and comics. Approximately 50-60 percent of major mass market sales is achieved
through this distribution system. The system,
begun in the late nineteenth century in response
to the monopoly the American News Company had
on national magazine distribution, was used by
Pocket Books beginning in 1941.

To reach these IDs, who today number approximately 450, paperback publishers established not only strong internal sales departments but also occasionally had ties with independent sales operations, national distributors already selling magazines and comics to the IDs. Publishers quickly learned that the best national distributors carried the bestselling magazines. Using the threat of reduced magazine allocations, these national distributors had the "muscle" to convince local IDs to handle larger monthly allotments of the book publishers they represented. Larger allotments usually meant more retail display space and, therefore, greater sales.

There are wide-ranging estimates for the average display life for a new paperback edition on a retail display rack, falling between seven days to two months. The trade journal of the book industry, PUBLISHERS WEEKLY, in 1975 estimated an average of 15 days. This figure is widely accepted. Regardless of the actual time, it is clear that the new softcover edition has to fight against great odds to remain visible at the retail level for more than a few weeks. The short display span directly contributes to the industry's extremely high return rate that approaches 50% of what it manufactures.

Publishers try to acquire reprint rights for at least five years. This allows them to reissue a book several times during the life of the contract. Reissues generally receive new cover designs and, depending on past paperback performance and any new factors that could affect sales, are redistributed with fresh marketing stratagems.

Distribution through local independent wholesalers, however, is by no means the only sales channel for paperbacks. Besides foreign and institutional sales, other types of accounts usually serviced directly by the publisher's

own sales force are large chain-store accounts
and the regular retail bookstore trade. In recent years the dramatic growth of direct book
sales in both of these areas encouraged the
largest of the paperback houses to withdraw
from sales arrangements with national distributor sales organizations and set up national
distributing arms of their own to service both
direct and wholesaler accounts.

Manufacturing

Recalling the technological advances in book-
making that supported the paperback revolutions
of the nineteenth century, adaptations and improvements in printing and binding became a
second element of modern paperback publishing
success. Improvements have allowed softcover
books to be made quickly and, most important,
cheaply. Paperback publishers found that prin-
ters of magazines, mail-order catalogs and other
graphic art materials, which were manufactured
in large quantities and had relatively short
life expectancies, were the best sources for
softcover manufacture.
    The use of high-speed rotary magazine
presses by softcover houses precedes the ad-
vent of Pocket Books which actually used book
presses to print its first editions. In 1937,
Modern Age Books were printed at the Rimford
Press on machinery designed for the READER'S
DIGEST. Following World War II, several book
manufacturers, i.e., those who set the type,
make the printing plates, print and bind the
books, expanded their paperback printing facili-
ties. Most notably, these were W. F. Hall in
Chicago, J. W. Clement (now Aracata Graphics) of
Buffalo and Western Printing and Lithographing
(now Western Publishing) of Racine, Wisconsin.
These companies continue to be the major manufacturers of paperback books in America.

The most dramatic improvement in the manufacture of paperbacks was made by the English
printing-press manufacturer, Strachan & Henshaw.
In 1951 it first delivered to W. F. Hall one of
its letterpress flexographic presses. This
press, which used flexible rubber printing
plates, required considerably less time to pre-
pare for printing (known as "make-ready" time)
and ran more than ten times faster than the rotary magazine presses and more than fifteen
times faster than the book press in Clinton,
Massachusetts, where the first Pocket Book titles
were made. Requiring thirty percent less ink
than more conventional letterpress methods, the
printed paper dried almost instantly, allowing
for folding, gathering and binding sheets at
speeds that matched the speed of the new presses.

Today, the vast majority of paperbacks are
still printed on flexographic equipment similar
to those in the early 1950s; however, as with
all types of printed material, offset printing,
which allows for greater use of internal illustration, has made great inroads into paperback
manufacture.

The binding of paperbacks has also been im-
proved. Early Pocket Books and Avon titles had
sewn signatures. Coverstock, more than fifty
percent thicker than today's wrappers, were
glued to endpapers and affixed to the untrimmed
spines. A piece of gauze-like cloth, "crash,"
between the cover and the signatures, served as
added binding support.

The sewn bindings disappeared during the
early years of World War II, however, and less
expensive "perfect" binding, a misnomer if there
ever was one, was substituted. Back spines were
trimmed during the binding process and a coating
of animal-based glue attached the cover to the
pages. This binding method, which can be traced
back to the nineteenth-century France, increased
binding speed approximately 800 percent over

conventional methods. It permitted assembly-
line production and kept pace with the speed of
rotary and flexographic presses.

Extreme temperature changes frequently resulted in the chemical breakdown of the animal-
based glue used in the perfect binding process.
The books fell apart. As early as 1944, experi-
ments were made with synthetic binding materials,
but not until the 1960s were publishers and manufacturers of paperbacks satisfied with the service and relative durability of the perfect
binding adhesives. During these two decades,
the unstable nature of the paperback binding re-
inforced the unsettled image softcover books
held in the eye of the American public.

The printing and binding improvements made
during the early years of mass market publishing
directly contributed to their relatively low
price. With few exceptions, paperback books
remained at the original twenty-five cent price
until the early 1950s when thicker thirty-five
cent, fifty cent and, eventually seventy-five
cent volumes were introduced. Although these
Extra, Giants, Specials, Double, and Triple
volumes became common, the majority of paperbacks published continued to carry a twenty-
five cent cover price through the mid-1950s.

People mistakenly believe that the cost
difference between a hardcover book and a paperback is in the binding. There are obvious savings in the cost of materials when one compares
the stiff paper cover of a softcover edition
with the boards and cloth of a sewn hardcover
book. However, these material savings alone do
not account for the $17.40 estimated by PUBLISH-
ERS WEEKLY in 1978 as the difference between
the average paperback price, $1.90, and that of
a hardcover book, $19.30.

The most significant factor affecting the
difference in price lies in the quantity of
books manufactured. The greater the press run,
the lower the per-unit cost to make them. For

instance, an average first novel may only have
a printing of 7,500 copies. Rarely are any mass
market paperbacks, originals or reprints, printed in quantities of less than 75,000. Most
first printings far exceed this figure. Outside
of the cost of paper, the per-unit cost to manufacture a 75,000-copy printing is much less
than that of a 7,500-copy edition. The use of
efficient high-speed technologies in composi-
tion, presswork and binding increases speed of
manufacture and reduces labor costs for each
copy made, thus permitting much lower cover
prices.

Today, initial print orders are determined
by the nature of the material being published,
but during the very early years of contemporary
paperback publishing this was not so. Most
titles received the same first printings. During World War II this was usually 100,000
copies for Pocket Books. By the spring of 1946,
however, THE NEW YORK TIMES BOOK REVIEW reported
that standard first printings for Pocket Books
and Bantam were 300,000; Dell, 150,000; Avon,
100,000; and Penguin and Pelicans 200,000 and
50,000, respectively.

Publishers soon began to discriminate between titles and types of publications, to "posi-
tion" their books on their monthly lists of new
releases. Pocket Books announced in 1947 that
it had started to rank titles at three levels
according to their sales potential. First-
ranked titles could receive a print order in
excess of 500,000 copies, while third-ranked
titles might be as low as 150,000.

Editorial Selection

A third element contributing to the success
of contemporary paperbacks is judicious editorial selection. A brief outline of the common
editorial trends and practices is required in

even the shortest history of American paperback publishing.

Pocket Books' experience with the mystery-detection category was not lost on the successful paperback houses that followed during the war years--Avon, Popular Library, and Dell. Popular Library's early publications were almost exclusively those of cloak-and-dagger **and** detection. The early Dell and Popular Library logos symbolized their commitment to the genre.

Often taking their cues from the pulp magazines of the day, other categories of popular literature gained regular rack space in the drugstores and newsstands of the 1940s. Pocket Books, with the unlikely title OH, YOU TEX, brought out its first western in the fall of 1940. Dell, Popular Library and, after the war, Bantam also took frequent aim at readers of this category.

Women's romances, pioneered by Dell, were also slow to get off the paperback presses. This changed in the late 1940s and early 1950s with publications of Pocket Books and Dell.

Science fiction was the last major category of popular literature to establish itself in paperback. Donald A. Wollheim edited THE POCKET BOOK OF SCIENCE FICTION in 1943, but relatively little more appeared until the early 1950s when Ace, Ballantine and others began publishing titles in this genre.

Fictionalized war stories written in a vein similar to successful adventure comic and pulp magazines of the 1940s and 1950s, never caught on in paperback form. Nonfiction war accounts, especially diaries and personal histories, however, were successful. These began with the Penguin Specials of World War II and continued with the World War II accounts published by Ballantine in the mid-1950s and reissued many times since then.

A readership survey taken in the early

41

1950s indicated that the paperback audience was
about evenly divided between male and female
readers. The fifties saw the beginning of an
industry-wide emphasis on female readership.
By the close of the 1970s women readers accoun-
ted for about two-thirds of mass market sales
and completely dominated some fiction categories.
Bestselling historical romances (labeled erotic
gothics or "bodice rippers" by some) find that
98 percent of their readership is female.
    Today, just as in the 1940s, paperback
publishers issue books monthly. Books con-
tracted for by the publisher are scheduled to
fill out the various slots on each monthly list.
The slots include lead titles (reprints of best-
sellers or books deemed to have paperback best-
seller potential), genre fiction (mysteries,
romance, westerns, science fiction), and mid-
list (a wide variety of new and reissued nonfiction and contemporary fiction). An assort-
ment of game, puzzle, cartoon and classic reprints usually fill out the monthly offerings
of a mass market house. Placing a new edition
into this scheme and prescribing appropriate
marketing efforts for it is termed "positioning."
    Most of a publisher's promotion, publicity
and advertising is directed toward each month's
lead books. The publisher takes into account
many factors when issuing these lead titles,
including the author's reputation, the type of
literature, the currency of the topic and the
success or lack of success experienced by the
original hardcover edition. Lists are drawn
up a half year or more in advance of publication.
As the month of publication approaches the final
lists are refined.
    Through the years, successful paperback
publishers have learned, frequently by speedily
published imitations of competitor successes,
what mix of titles seems most saleable. Their
monthly lists reflect careful analysis of read-

ing habits. Trends, particularly those surroun-
ding category fiction, are divined; past sales
analyzed. Some editorial innovations, such as
recent trend in multivolume historical sagas,
require years of development and hundreds of
thousands of dollars to develop. Others, like
the "Happy Hooker" accounts of the early 1970s,
are relatively short-lived. The first paperback appearance of a widely publicized bestselling, lead title frequently finds paperback
publishers reissuing in fresh cover designs earlier publications of the same writer. Some lead
titles are determined to be "blockbusters."
Generally, these are books for which the reprinter has paid a sizeable advance. For blockbusters, all the stops may be pulled, with ex-
tensive radio, television, newspaper and magazine advertising employed. Until the late 1970s
it was rare that an original mass market paperback was designated as a lead title.

Two separate but interrelated editorial
patterns have emerged from the forty-plus years
paperback publishers have issued genre literature. The first is the cyclical nature of the
popular categories. Mysteries, westerns and
romances have experienced times when sales
dropped off and publishers have responded by
reducing the number issued or eliminating the
category completely.

The other pattern is the tendency of various ficitonal categories to subdivide and become more specialized as their number of readers
increases. Mysteries, for instance, developed
into detective and hardboiled detective fiction,
spy and intrigue fiction and gothic and horror
tales, as well as classic "who-done-its." Romances have splintered into doctor and nurse
books, gothic romance and romantic suspense,
historical romance and the various period romances, e.g., Regency and Victorian.

Each subcategory of popular fiction has its
own core of regular readers on which accurate

sales predictions can generally be made month-in and month-out. Because of this, first printing orders within these subcategories vary little from one title to the next. Many monthly lists of paperback publications are made up of two-thirds to three-fourths of category fiction.

Generally, nonfiction sales are much more difficult to predict; however, once titles achieve successful sales levels they frequently become staples of a publisher's backlist and attract seasonal, school and college sales. Nonfiction mass market paperbacks commonly are reprints of bestselling titles, how-to-do-it books or original publications covering topical subjects or popular personalities.

Usually made up of fictional titles and often in the public domain (i.e., a publication is no longer covered by copyright and permission to publish is not required), classic series such as the Washington Square imprint of Pocket Books and the Signet Classic and Bantam Pathfinder series attract the same kind of institutional interest. Other types of publications likely to appear on a publisher's list of new monthly releases are cookbooks and puzzle books, as well as cartoon books and, frequently before each new school year, one or more reference works.

Paperback publishers accept few "unsolicited" manuscripts for publication. Literary agents usually link the author of an original manuscript with a paperback publisher. It is an agent's business to know which paperback publishers are most inclined to consider their writer's works. Agents commonly receive a commission of ten percent of the author's advance and subsequent royalty payments.

Upon acceptance of a manuscript, a paperback publisher, while retaining paperback rights, may "farm it out," i.e., place it with a hardcover publishing house. Many major paperback houses have their own original hardcover or trade paperback publishing programs and may choose to issue a trade edition under one of their own imprints.

Approximately sixty percent of today's mass market paperbacks are reprints of hardcover originals, however, and usually are published by another company. Softcover publsihers spend much time and effort reviewing the submissions of hardcover publishers who will on occasion delay making a final commitment for publicaiton to authors and their agents until a paperback reprinter has been lined up. Generally, the advance paid by a paperback reprinter is split fifty-fifty between an author and the hardcover publisher.

The publishing chronicles of the 1970s are splashed with the red and black ink of massive publishing advances. Best known are the $1,800,000 paid by Bantam to E. L. Doctorow and his hardcover publisher Random House for RAGTIME, the $2,500,000 paid by Avon to Colleen McCullough and Harper & Row for THE THORN BIRDS, and the $2,240,000 paid by New American Library for Mario Puzo's Putnam hardcover edition of FOOLS DIE and reissue rights to THE GODFATHER. In the fall of 1979 Bantam shelled out a record $3.2 million for the softcover rights to the then-unpublished Judith Krantz novel, PRINCESS DAISY. The practice of bidding huge sums on unpublished works is a phenomenon of the later 1970s and would not have been dreamed of twenty years earlier.

Format

The final element that contributed to the success of mass market paperback publishing is the physical format of the book itself. Of all of the contributions Robert de Graff and Pocket Books made to the successful establishment of mass market paperback book publishing in the

United States, least understood and appreciated
is the manner in which the original Pocket Books
format contributed to the industry's success.
Although all of the design features that De
Graff incorporated in his original book design
were inspired by previous European and American
hardcover and paperback publications, the happy
combination of physical size, weight, shape,
page design, appealing logo and bright, attrac-
tive cover art and graphics produced a package
that eventually captured the mass market for the
softcover book. This image is so strong that
even today the American public frequently refers
to all paperbacks, both trade and mass market,
as "pocket books."
     The dimensions of today's rack-size paper-
back, approximately 4 1/2" x 7 1/8", are dicta-
ted, among other things, by the width of a paperback display pocket. Pocket Books' original
dimensions, 4 1/8" x 6 1/2", were more compact
than the foreign Albatross and Penguin series.
With the exception of New American Library,
early U. S. mass market paperbacks used printing
equipment that accomodated either height, and
the per-unit price difference between the two
seems to have been insignificant.
     The conversion from the smaller to the
larger size became significant in 1953 when
Bantam switched to the longer format, joining
NAL, Fawcett and Ballantine with 7 1/8" books.
The longer dimension more closely resembled
poster art proportions, the basic style of cover illustration that was beginning to evolve.
     The impelling reason for dimension conver-
sion, however, lay outside the publisher's door,
at the point of sale, the retail display rack.
Throughout the 1940s and early 1950s, paperback
books were arranged by publisher and publisher
imprint instead of the subject and category
arrangements one finds in today's retail outlets.
The growth in the number of paperback publica-

tions in print, together with proof that retailers better pleased their public and sold more books when titles were arranged by subject and category, led to mixing paperback imprints on the same display units. Publishers of the stubbier paperbacks discovered that they literally were being overshadowed by the taller imprints. By the mid-1960s the 6 1/2" height was dropped by all major publishers.

The most interesting and eye-catching aspect of the paperback format, however, is the cover design and artwork, a subject frequently addressed in the pages of this journal. Its evolution from book jacket and magazine cover roots has been and will continue to be the subject for numerous future explorations. My book, scheduled for publication by Penguin in 1982, UNDERCOVER: AN ANNOTATED HISTORY OF AMERICAN PAPERBACKS, will also deal with paperback cover art and design history, evolution and contemporary practice in some detail.

The World's Great Novels of Detection
(Selected by Anthony Boucher)
by Don Hensley

In 1965 Bantam introduced a very interest-ing and very short-lived series called "The World's Great Novels of Detection." This series featured five mysteries selected by famous cri-tic and writer Anthony Boucher.

Each one of the books has an introduction by Mr. Boucher which explains why he chose it for the series. The front cover uses a puzzle-like effect which is very original and distinc-tive (similar to the the cover design of the current Murder Ink and Scene of the Crime series by Dell; see PQ III/4). But the real treat comes on the back cover which has a black and white drawing (map) of the scene of the crime. Although these drawings are not as detailed as the Dell mapbacks of a previous era, it is nice to see someone try this concept one more time.

Another feature of this series is on the first page, the top half of which lists some of the characters in the book; the bottom half has critical blurbs to further entice the reader.

This short series is very collectible. Recently a dealer was selling the complete set of five for $17.50. Not bad for a series that's only seventeen years old.

Here's a list of the five books that make up "The World's Great Novels of Detection" series:

1. CAT OF MANY TAILS, Ellery Queen. In the introduction Anthony Boucher calls this one of the seven best books written by Ellery Queen.

2. GREEN FOR DANGER, Christinna Brand. Mr. Boucher considers this one a tricky puzzler that "is so neatly misleading."

3. CUE FOR MURDER, Helen McCloy. This is a very exciting "whodunit" thriller featuring Dr. Basil Willing.

rim
of the
pit

HAKE TALBOT

A BANTAM MYSTERY F2922 ★ ★ 50¢

A MASTERPIECE OF DETECTIVE WIZARDRY
AND SUPERNATURAL MURDER!

4.   A BLUNT INSTRUMENT, Georgette Heyer. Although more famous as a writer of Regency romances, Ms. Heyer does a fine job with this case of a missing murder weapon.

5.   RIM OF THE PIT, Hake Talbot. Mr. Boucher compares RIM OF THE PIT favorably with the best of John Dickson Carr as a novel of mystery and the supernatural.

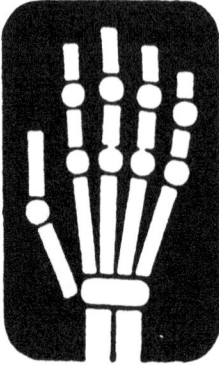

Colophon used for "The Worlds Great Novels of Detection" series

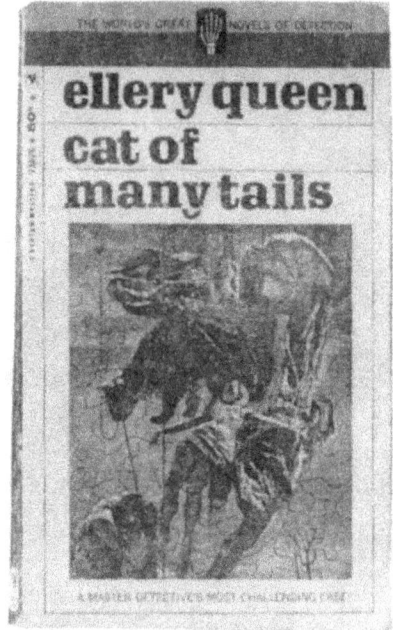

Top portion of back cover of *Cat of Many Tails* featuring a map characteristic of the series

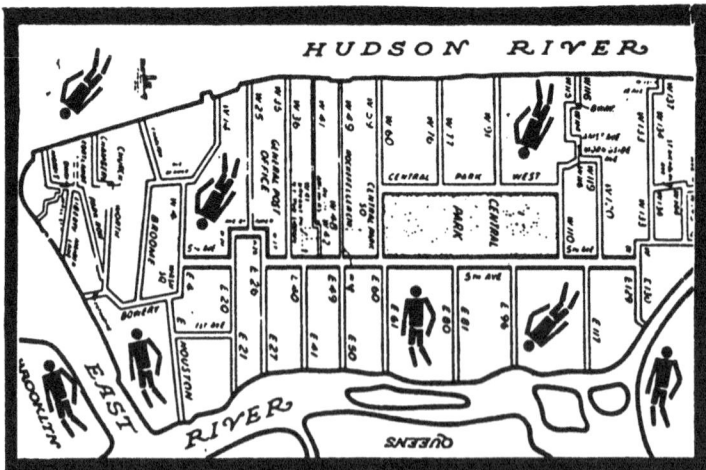

Notes & Letters

Ellen Nehr, from her Bexley, Ohio, Den of Arcane Paperback Lore, has informed the editors that the Norman Daniels checklist (PQ Fall 1981) lists only one novel by Daniels under the "James Clayford" name. This name was also used on the following books: RECKLESS! and RESPECT-ABLE from Venus Books, and CARELESS!, SINFUL!, MARRIAGE CAN WAIT, WEEK-END GIRL, LURE FOR LOVE, BED TIME GIRL, and ILLICIT WIFE from Quarter Books. These were all digest-sized publications.

> Mike Barson responds: On authority of the Copyright Office registrations and Norman Daniels himself, these other James Clayford books were not written by Daniels. James Clayford must have been a house name.

★ ★ ★

Steve Stilwell has provided contributing editor Bill Crider with a copy of POWERFUL PASSION (Novel Books, 1961) by John Jakes. This book was not included on the John Jakes check list in the Fall 1980 PQ.

★ ★ ★

Dear Charlotte,
Enclosed is a list of the Flagship titles I have been able to track down. My interest stemed from Jim Sanderson's list in the Fall 1979 issue. There seem to have been at least 64 books published. They were published in 1967 and 1968 and the number (7xx or 8xx) seems to refer to the year. I am pretty sure that the CDC on the spines of the first 8 books are the initials of the distributor but I don't know what they stand for.
I think I've found all the 'easy' books and that filling in the gaps is going to be very difficult. Any help would be appreciated.

Partial List of Flagship Books:

701 CDC 060 THE PLOT by K.P. Kelley
702 CDC 060 PINK DOLPHIN by P.T. Olemy
703 CDC 060 DEAD MAN OUT by C.B. Gilford
704 CDC 060 PORTRAIT IN FEAR by Vera Henry
705
706
707 CDC 060 A PRESENT FOR HARRY by Maury
               Campbell
708 CDC 060 A MAN CALLED BLACK by Will
               Manson
092-00709-075   THE TRANSGRESSORS by P.T. Olemy
092-00710-075   TURN YOUR BACK ON HEAVEN*
092-00711-060   THE RUNNER IS RED by J.R.
                 Kovalsky
        712
092-00713-075   HOW TO CONTROL ARTHRITIS by
                 Dr. Giraud W. Campbell
092-00714-075   IN PRAISE OF LOVE by Cole
                 Freedman
092-00715-060   MOONSPIN by Elmer J. Carpenter
092-00716-060   THE MATHEMATICIAN by Will Manson
        717
        718
092-00719-060   BRAVO 9 by Will B. Day
        720
        721
092-00722-075   VALLEY OF THE MOON GODDESS by
                 J. Thomas Homsby
092-00723-060   A DEADLY GAME by Will Manson
        724
        725
        726
092-00727-060   THE EARLY DAYS OF AUGUST by
                 J.R. Kovalsky
092-00728-060   MALACHI BREEN TIMES 2 by Leo
                 Pope
092-00729-075   TO HELL-OR CONNAUGHT**
        730-075 THERAPEUTIC SELF-HYPNOSIS by
                 William C. Gibson

092-00731-060	THE CHINESE CONUNDRUN by Will Manson
732	
092-00734-075	A STRANGER TO THE DEED by Walter Cummins
092-00734-075	A JADE MANDELAINE by David B. Churchill
092-00735-060	THE MAN FROM M.O.D. by Will B. Day
36	
37	
092-00838-075	INTO TEMPTATION by Walter Cummins
092-00839-060	THE DANGEROUS ONES by Will Manson
092-00840-060	THE CLONES by P.T. Olemy
841	
092-00842-075	THE KEEPER by Howard Le Roy
092-00843-060	LOVE SPY, LOVE by Roy Charles Kasper
844	
845	
092-00846-060	LAY-OVER TOWN by Dan Brennan
092-00847-060	A TOUCH OF MURDER by J.B. Cearley
848	
849	
850	
851	
092-00852-060	THE DUKE by Will Manson
092-00 853-095	THE MIRACLE WITHIN YOU***
092-00 854-075	RUN FOR THE WAVES****
855	
092-00856-060	MURDER...IN FULL VIEW by J.D. Forbes
857	
092-00858-075	CYNTHIA by Jack Avreen
092-00859-060	THE SPUR OF FEAR by Eric Hammond Manring
092-00860-060	A VERY BLACK DEED by Will Manson
861	

```
        862
        863
092-00864-060        EXILE AND OTHER TALES OF FANTASY
                     by M.A. Cummings
```

    *by Carl Post
   **by Patrick B. Parkes
  ***by John Myers
 ****by William C. Leikam

                    best,
                    Bill Denholm
                    184 Centre St. Apt #5
                    Mountain View, CA 94041

                    ★ ★ ★

Dear Billy,
    I enjoyed Volume IV, #3 especially Charley
Culpepper's detailed study of Pocket Books.
However the article mistakenly notes that Modern
Age Books discontinued paperbacks after 1939.
The article on John Esteven in PQ Volume IV, #2
made the same error. Although Modern Age's
emphasis shifted to hardcovers after 1939, the
firm published new paperback titles through 1942,
as well as issuing later printings of earlier
releases.
                    Best wishes,
                    Bill O'Connell
                    204 West 88th St.
                    New York, N.Y. 10024

                    ★ ★ ★

Dear PQ gang,
    About Bill Crider's "SF Writers in Other
Fields" [PQ vol IV, #3], there were two Lancer
printings of A WHIFF OF DEATH: 74-545 (75¢) and
447-75315-095 (95¢). Lancer was doing the
paperback edition of the Walker & Company hardcover. I am told that in the second book of his
autobiography, Asimov makes some reference to

Walker using the original title (his) since it was Avon that changed it to THE DEATH DEALERS. This should be easy to check but I have not yet read the second book.

I will be sending Al Grossman a post card but for your information, "CM" [see PQ vol IV, #3 page 50] is Charles Moll, who got his start selling covers to Lancer.

I found Mike Barson's Norman Daniels [PQ vol IV, #3] info very interesting.

best,
Bill Denholm
184 Centre St. Apt 5
Mountain View, CA 94041

Book Sellers

The following people sell paperbacks. Many mail out booklists and all are knowledgeable paperback bibliophiles. For Specific wants write directly to the addresses below and please include S.A.S.E.

Bill & Pat Lyles
77 High St.
Greenfield, MA 01301
(413) 774-2432

Scott Owen
P.O. Box 343
Moraga, CA 94556

Gravesend Books
Box 235
Poconopines, PA 18350

Anthony Smith
1414 Lynnview Dr.
Houston, TX 77055

PCI
P.O. Box 1308
Hawaiian Gardens, CA 97016

Jeff Meyerson
50 First Place
Brooklyn, N.Y. 11231

Jack Irwin
16 Gloucester Lane
Trenton, N.J. 08618

Fantasy Archives
71 Eight Ave.
New York, N.Y. 10014

Bill Lippincott
Dunbar Hill Rd.
North Anson, ME 04958

Michael Barson
117 Crosby St.
Haverhill, MA 01830

Beasley Books
1533 W. Oakdale, 2nd Fl.
Chicago, IL 60657

Family Paperbacks
4016 Central Ave. N.E.
Minneapolis, MN 55412

Sign of the Unicorn Book Shop
604 Kingstown Rd.
Peace Dale, RI 02883

Abra-Cadaver
The House of Mystery
110 Dunrovin Lane
Rochester, N.Y. 14618

Remember When Shop
2433 Valwood Pkwy.
Dallas, TX 75234

Ed Kalb
3227 E. Enid Ave.
Mesa, Arizona 85204
(602) 830-1855

Jeff Patton
3621 Carolina St., N.W.
Massillon, OH 44646

McClintock Books
P.O. Box 3111
Warren, OH 44485

Fantastic Worlds Bookstore
4816 A Camp Bowie Blvd.
Fort Worth, Texas 76107

Paperback Paradise
468 Centre St.
Jamaica Plain, MA 02130

Gorgon Books
21 Deerlane
Wantagh, N.Y. 17793

The Old Book Store
210 E. Cuyahoga Falls Ave.
Akron, OH 44310

Murder By The Book
194½ Atwells Ave.
Providence, RI 02903

The Odyssey Shop
1743 S. Union Ave.
Alliance, OH 44601

Larry Rickert
R.D. 1 Box 56C
Augusta, NJ 07822

John Da Prato
61 Puffer Lane
Sudbury, MA 01776

Lone Wolf Mysteries
160 Pennsylvania Ave.
Mt. Vernon, N.Y. 10552

Ralph Kristiansen
P.O. Box 524-Kenmore Station
Boston, MA 02215

Bunker Books
P.O. Box 1638
Spring Valley, CA 92077
(714) 469-3296

Gale Sebert
Sebert's Books
Leivasy, WV 26676

JOHN HARTLING
1124 Galloway
Columbia, TN 38401

Ron Czerwien
7289 W. 173rd Pl.
Tinley Park, IL 60477

R.C. & ELWANDA HOLLAND
302 Martin Dr.
Richmond, KY 40475

Keith & Martin Book Shop
310 W. Franklin St.
Chapel Hill, N.C. 27514

Tom Nigra
865 Diane Court
Woodbridge, NJ 07095
(201) 634-7105

C.D. DUNCAN
Box 9802 Suite 122
Austin, TX 78766

JACKS BOOK SHOP
718 E. Northwest Hwy.
Mt. Prospect, IL 60056

Lucile Coleman
P.O. Box 610813
North Miami, FL 33161

Pandora's Books LTD
Box 86
Neche, ND 58265

Diamond Lake Book Store
1 West Diamond Lake Rd.
Minneapolis, Minn. 55419

Mostly Mysteries Books
398 St. Clair Avenue East
Toronto, Ontario M4T 1P5

The Book Bin
323 Parkdale Center
Waco, Texas 76710
(817) 776-4743

BECKY ICAZA
33 Spring Park Ave.
Jamaica Plain, MA 02130

COLE SPRINGER
P.O. Box 650
Times Square Station
N.Y., N.Y. 10108

If you are a bookseller and would like your name and address printed in "Book Sellers," please drop us a line. Please tell us if you sell paperbacks by mail and/or have a retail store.

★ ★ ★ ★ ★

Paperback quarterly is available for retail distribution by bookstores or mail order dealers. An order of ten copies(minimum) costs $15.00 and retails for $29.50 ($2.95 each). All unsold copies are returnable at dealers expense for refund. Payment must accompany orders except for standing orders which will be billed. Write to *Paperback Quarterly*, 1710 Vincent, Brownwood, Texas 76801.

The American Paperback Institute
1710 Vincent Street
Brownwood, Texas 76801

Designed and compiled by Piet Schreuders (author of *Paperbacks, U.S.A.*), the American Paperback Calendar is printed in red and black ink featuring unique graphics using 2-color overlap.

The calendar measures approximately 10½ by 16½ inches with a spiral binding for easy handling.

All months except July and October feature actual size cover reproductions of 2 covers by collectable paperback cover artists. Each month gives a summary about the artist(s) featured.

Jan: Gerald Gregg
Feb: Rafael DeSoto and
 Robert McGinnis
March: Rudolph Belarski
April: Leo Manso
May: Arthur Getz and
 Michael Loew
June: Isador N. Steinberg
July: Stanley Meltzoff
Aug: Robert Jonas
Sept: Stanley Zuckerberg
Oct: Popular Library's
 title page covers
Nov: H. Lawrence Hoffman
Dec: E. McKnight and
 James Avati

Rudolph Belarski showing off a galley proof of American Paperback Calendar 1982 -- Westport, Conn. Oct. 26, 1981

Bookseller, Robert Weinberg says, The 1982 American Paperback
Calendar is..."*a very nice item for a paperback collector...One
of the best fan publications we have ever handled (fan in the
sense that it has been done by fans -- it is entirely professional in
every aspect -- typeset, etc. etc.) Obviously, very highly rec-
ommended.*"

Now being mailed in tube mailers!

American Paperback Calendar
1710 Vincent   **Calendar $6.95 each**
Brownwood, Texas 76801   **Postage Paid**

Order Today --- Limited Quanity Available

Dear Mr. Lee:

Thanks for sending the first issue of PAPERBACK QUARTERLY, which seems an admirable venture for the fan and collector of paperbacks. It should also do well as a vehicle for collating and correcting the history of the paperback books, as such.

Re your Query #4, on page 43, I think I can answer this as I was the editor of Avon Books at the time. The designation "Novel Library" was adopted at Avon to create a new series of books of light adult-romance (i.e. Moderately sexy, as things went in those days) novels. The Jack Woodford novels were all bought by Avon, but as time went on, it was decided to do most of them under the Novel Library imprint. I believe all these were reprints from books done in hardcovers during the 1920's and 1930's. All were somewhat abridged--mainly for Woodford's peculiar political ravings and filler-asides, not for sex which they had only teaser references to. All these books were 25¢. I imagine the 35¢ prices you note may have been later editions, but my memory is inexact on this.

Re you wants, p. 44: There was no Avon Fantasy Monthly. The correct title was Avon Fantasy Reader. There was no Ace edition of THE HOBBITT.

Cordially,
Donald A. Wollheim
DAW BOOKS, INC.
New York, New York

Gentlemen:

PQ is handsomely done.

Notes & Queries #2: This is hardly surprising. Paperback books are made up of 16 page signatures so any book will have some multiple of 16 pages. What is odd is that you found so many with 192. I assume that you have the small rather than the standard size. A very common page count for standard size pb's is 160 pages. Some books have as few as 128 but such a book is rather slim. Some publishers will reset a book in larger type when it is reissued at a higher price to

make the buyer think he is getting his "money's worth"
(a fat book).

On page 20 there is a reference to the Ace series
of Conan books. At the time, 1967, the series was
being published by Lancer.

I wish you well with your venture and will give
serious thought to submitting a contribution.

Sincerely,
William J. Denholm III
Mountain View, California

————————————

Dear Readers,

Thank you for all your comments both
pro and con. We enjoy feed back from our
readers to enable us to better gage what
type of publication you want.

Our aim is to improve both the quality
of articles and reproductions in each issue.
Naturally the editors own interests and
experiences make it difficult to cover all
areas of the paperback industry well. If
you are knowledgeable in a particular area
of paperback collecting, we urge you to
submit an article or note for possible
publication. We particularly want articles
dealing with cover illustrators.

------Billy C. Lee

PAPERBACK WRITERS
------Bill Crider .

It's ironic that John Faulkner, a minor but nevertheless interesting, capable, and entertaining writer, should be known best to students of literature for a book called My Brother Bill, a remiscence of William, the infinitely more famous member of the Faulkner family. One probable reason for John's relative obscurity is the fact that his last five novels appeared as paperback originals. These books, in the order of their publication, are Cabin Road (1951), Uncle Good's Girls (1952), The Sin Shouter of Cabin Road (1955), Ain't Gonna Rain No More (1959), and Uncle Good's Week-End Party (1960). All were originally published by Fawcett Gold Medal, though Cabin Road has since been reprinted in hardback (1969) and paperback by the prestigious Louisiana State University Press. As the First book in the series, Cabin Road probably sold the most copies and went through at least five printings at Gold Medal, three in 1951 alone, one in 1954, and one in 1958.

Before launching into a series of generalizations about the books, I should admit that I have seen only four of them. Although I've searched for years, I've been unable to find a copy of Uncle Good's Girls. Ironically, this book was the only one of the series to be reviewed in a mass-circulation periodical (Newweek, June 23, 1952). I've read the review, and what I say about the books in general is likely (but not necessarily) true of Uncle Good's Girls.

The novels are set in the Mississippi backwoods country, so far back in the hills that civilization has barely penetrated (if it has penetrated at all). Life is lived by the characters who inhabit the shacks and cabins on a very basic and elemental level. Most conveniences (electricity, plumbing) are unknown, as are most necessities (cash money). Pleasures are simple-- seeing an automobile from one's front porch, for example, is an event of the first magnitude.

There is a quality of oral story-telling in all the books. The same tales (such as the loss of Uncle Good's well bucket or the escapades of the preacher)

8

are repeated again and again, as good stories always are. There is very little plotting involved. One event leads to another through a series of comic scenes until things have run their course and the book winds down, much as if the story-teller has run out of tales (temporarily). So he stops, until taking up the thread of the characters' lives another time. Most of the books involve the same characters who wander in and out of the story more or less at random and play roles of greater or lesser importance. This episodic structure is not necessarily a flaw. In fact, it adds to the books' haphazard, shaggy dog charm.

The humor of the series is the primary reason for its success. It is by turns bawdy, naive, knowing, and grotesque. In this regard, it is difficult to avoid comparisons with Erskine Caldwell, a better writer than many are willing to admit, who also had a sharp eye for the humor in the situations he described. Too, Faulkner (like Caldwell) owes a lot of his success to his frank emphasis on sex, though he uses sex almost exclusively as a basis for humor. The books seem almost Victorian by today's standards, but in the 1950s they were undoubtedly thought of as quite racy.

Most of the sexy episodes concern Jewel Mae and Orta June, Uncle Good's daughters. They work in Uncle Good's back bedroom and charge 50¢ a trick. Jones Peabody, who never has 50¢, tries to get a turn on credit from the first book to the last, but Uncle Good is a firm believer in business on a cash basis. By the time of Uncle Good's Week-End Party, Orta June's price has gone up to 55¢, owing to Uncle Good's belief that she is "livelier" than her sister. This belief arose because "Orta June had thrown one man clear off the cot and over against the wall one day" (p. 72; all page numbers refer to the first Gold Medal editons of the work being quoted). In reality, Orta June had thrown the man off in an attempt to reach Toodie (Jewel Mae's three-year-old son), who had raked a stick across her newly painted toenails as she was in the process of earning 50¢.

Toodie remains three years old from the beginning of the series to the end. His claim to fame is that

he drinks and cusses just like a man. He also has
incredible powers of urination, which Uncle Good de-
lights in showing off: "'Git over there to the edge
of the porch and show 'em how fur you can pee, Toodie.
Go on. Show 'em'" (Cabin Road, pp. (sic)106-107).
When Jewel Mae takes offense at the crudity of her
father, he is likely to retaliate: "'Go pee on your
maw, Toodie'" (p. 107).

   Orta June herself is not described in detail, but
judging from her effect on men, she must have been
quite a looker. In The Sin Shouter of Cabin Road, a
trucker named Frank sees her with her wrapper open and
is transfixed: "Frank's face was beet-red and slowly
turning purple. His eyes could be raked off with a
stick" (p. 67).

   Everyone in these books is interested in sex, even
the preacher, whose primary interest in life seems to
be in swapping tutti-frutti gum to any woman around
for a little sex. In Cabin Road, Jones Peabody even
resorts to tying his wife to himself with a plowline,
but he takes a nap and wakes up to find her calmly
chewing tutti-frutti. In discussing the preacher with
his black neighbors, Ex-Senator and Equator, Jones
observes that "'Hit looks like he ought to git enough
sometime.'" But Ex-Senator, whose wife also chews a
lot of gum, replies, "'Dey ain't dat much'" (p. 30).

   Despite the preacher's peccadilloes, the people
in the area of Cabin Road still respect his calling.
In fact, his annual sermon on fornication is one of
the highlights of the year. In The Sin Shouter of
Cabin Road, a brush arbor is built, and people from
miles around (including the foot washers) gather to
hear the preacher's message. He begins with an attack
on dancing:

          "They begin dancing with men. And the
          devil knowed they would. They put their
          pyore young bellies up ag'in the bellies
          of the evil men. And the devil knowed
          they'd do hit. And did they stop there?
          Jest aru-bing belly to belly with the
          lustful men?

"No!" shouted the man beside Jones.
"Tell hit, Preacher! Tell hit!" (p. 137)

It takes the preacher awhile, but he finally tells it, finally says what the crowd (now in a near frenzy of religious lust) has been waiting for:

"And what about that pyore young girl
when hit's all over?"

"What's all over?"

"She's done been fornicated!"

It was the word they had come to hear. They had been waiting for it.

"Wow-ee!" some man yelled again.

The men began jumping up and sitting down.
They slapped each other on the back as
hard as they could. . . . What women still
on their chairs now fell off. Nearly all
of them began talking in the Unknown
Tongue. . . . Davey had his wife about
the waist, trying to drag her out into
the bushes (pp. 141-142).

Of course, sex wasn't the only source of Faulkner's humor. In Ain't Gonna Rain No More, the weather plays a major part. The ground around Cabin Road is so dry and hard that it is impossible by bury Mr. Edgar, a recently deceased resident. Shovels make no mark on the earth. Picks make only small blue dents. No one is able to figure out what to do about Mr. Edgar until Ex-Senator suggests that they borrow Mr. Cronwell's tractor, which is equipped with a posthole digger. Most of the men agree to this idea, even though it means that Mr. Edgar will have to be buried upright, but even this method proves unsatisfactory. The digger only goes down six feet, and Mr. Edgar's height was over six feet, three inches. He is finally buried with

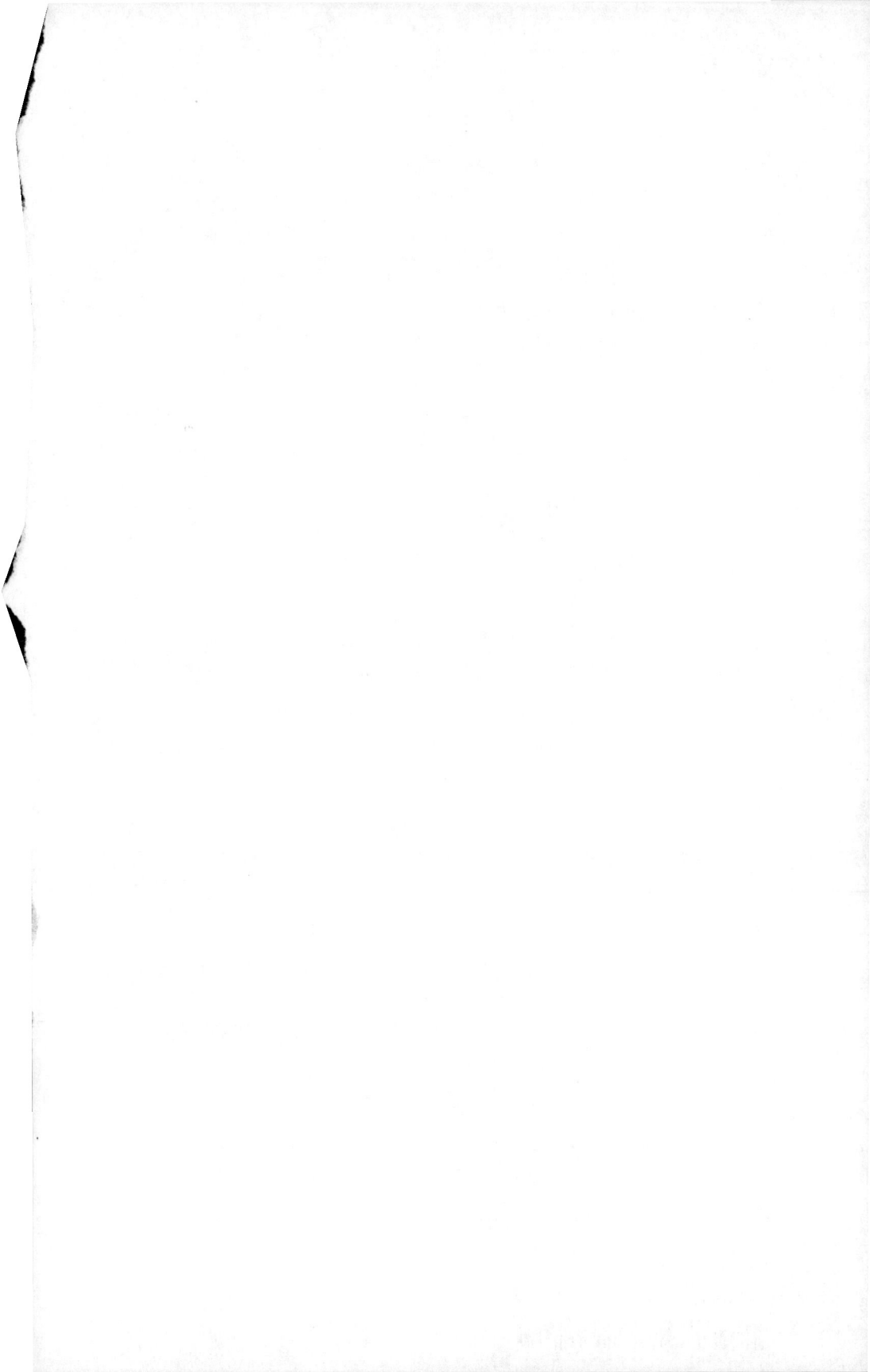

www.ingramcontent.com/pod-product-compliance
Lightning Source LLC
Chambersburg PA
CBHW021224020426
42331CB00003B/456